THE ILLUSTRATED POETS

THE ILLUSTRATED POETS

John Keats

Selected and with an introduction
by Geoffrey Moore

AURUM PRESS

First published 1991 by Aurum Press Limited,
25 Bedford Avenue, London WC1B 3AT
Selection and introduction copyright © 1991 by Geoffrey Moore

British Library Cataloguing in Publication Data

Keats, John *1795–1821*
John Keats. – (The illustrated poets).
I. Title II. Moore, Geoffrey *1920–* III. Series
821.7

ISBN 1 85410 169 2

3 5 7 9 10 8 6 4
1995

Picture research by Juliet Brightmore

Typeset by Computerset, Harmondsworth, Middlesex
Manufactured in China by Imago

CONTENTS

Introduction   10

'In drear-nighted December'   13
'Happy is England! I could be content'   14
On First Looking into Chapman's Homer   16
On the Grasshopper and Cricket   17
On the Sea   18

From ENDYMION: A Poetic Romance   20

'When I have fears that I may cease to be'   25

From HYPERION: A Fragment   26

Fancy   31
La Belle Dame sans Merci   36
Ode to Psyche   40
Ode to a Nightingale   44
Ode on a Grecian Urn   49
'Bright star, would I were stedfast as thou art'   53
Ode on Melancholy   54
To Autumn   57
'This living hand, now warm and capable'   60

Notes   61

INTRODUCTION

John Keats was born on 31 October 1795 and died on 23 February 1821, eight months before his twenty-sixth birthday. In that short space of time he produced work of greater quality than many other notable poets have achieved in double his life-span.

From the first, his life was dogged by tragedy and illness. His father, the manager of a livery stable, was killed in a riding accident when Keats was eight; his mother died of tuberculosis when he was fourteen. From the family home in Moorfields, Keats was sent to Clarke's school in Enfield and at the age of fifteen was apprenticed by his grandmother to an apothecary-surgeon. The eldest of five children, he had a particularly close relationship with his brother George, to whom some of his best letters were written.

Keats's letters are the wonder of the age. They are of as much interest as the poems themselves, and it is quite remarkable that a very young man could have produced such wisdom and insight. His famous doctrine of Negative Capability, put forward in a letter to George and Tom when he was twenty-two years old, defines it as the state in which a poet is 'capable of being in uncertainties, mysteries, doubts, without any irritable reaching after fact and reason'. This is the cast of mind which he said Shakespeare possessed 'so enormously' – and which, we might add, he also possessed when he wrote the great Odes.

These poems, which have added so much to English literature, were written when he was dying of tuberculosis and nursing his brother, who had the same disease. Keats's life is, in fact, a paradox. As a tuberculosis sufferer, he should have been a will-o'-the-wisp, but he was in fact sturdy and pugnacious, despite his height of only five feet one inch. Like his protagonist in the 'Ode on Melancholy', he 'burst Joy's grape against his palate fine'. Of all the great Romantic poets he is the most sensuous, without ever lapsing into the sensual, for his nature was at the same time pure and fine.

Before he developed his idolatry of Shakespeare, Keats was much drawn to Spenser. From all the evidence, his sure-footed 'Imitation of Spenser' was probably written early in 1814, when he was just nineteen. In 1815 he enrolled as a medical student at Guy's Hospital, becoming licensed to practise as an apothecary in 1816.

Keats's first major work, *Endymion*, was begun on 18 April 1817, at Carisbrooke on the Isle of Wight. On 8 October in that year he wrote to his friend Benjamin Bailey that he was going to make it 'a trial of my Powers of Imagination . . . by which I must take 4000 Lines of one bare circumstance and fill them with Poetry'. At this stage he still favoured the heroic couplet, which he forsook the next year for the Miltonic blank verse of *Hyperion*.

His brother Tom died in December 1818, while Keats was working on *Hyperion*. In the meantime he had fallen hopelessly in love with Fanny Brawne, who may have inspired 'The Eve of St Agnes'.

In April 1819 Keats wrote 'La Belle Dame sans Merci' and 'Ode to Psyche' and, later in the same year, the 'Ode on a Grecian Urn', 'Ode on Melancholy', 'Ode to a Nightingale' and 'To Autumn'. By that time his medical training told him that there was little which could save him from terminal illness.

On 3 February 1820 he noted that he was coughing arterial blood, the first unmistakable sign of the disease that was to kill him. He sailed to Italy in September, hoping that a milder climate might effect at least some temporary improvement, but alas it did not, and he lingered only a few more months.

In his lifetime Keats had to suffer brutal and unwarranted criticism. He was labelled by Lockhart in *Blackwood's* a member of the 'Cockney School' and both *Endymion* and *Hyperion* were savagely attacked. Although deeply wounded, Keats wrote to George, 'I think I shall be among the English Poets after my death.'

And so he is. Poets as divergent as Tennyson, Arnold and Hopkins all attested to the influence of Keats's poetry on them. He does not, like Shelley, soar into the empyrean but gives us something which is in the end more satisfying. His poetry is a continual celebration of life. When he saw a sparrow pecking about on the gravel, he did not merely identify himself with the bird, he became it.

When we read Keats's poems, we become him. We empathize not merely with his sentiments but with the whole man, for in his power to subdue his own ego, Keats raises us above the petty and the trivial. 'The roaring of the wind is my wife,' he wrote to George and Georgiana Keats in October 1818, 'and the Stars through the window pane are my Children.' How much more apt and fitting an epitaph this is than his own self-deprecating 'Here lies one whose name was writ in water.'

GEOFFREY MOORE

I

In drear-nighted December,
    Too happy, happy tree,
Thy Branches ne'er remember
    Their green felicity:
  The north cannot undo them,
  With a sleety whistle through them;
  Nor frozen thawings glue them
    From budding at the prime.

II

In drear-nighted December,
    Too happy, happy Brook,
Thy bubblings ne'er remember
    Apollo's summer look;
  But with a sweet forgetting,
  They stay their crystal fretting,
  Never, never petting
    About the frozen time.

III

Ah! would 'twere so with many
    A gentle girl and boy!
But were there ever any
    Writh'd not of passed joy?
  The feel of not to feel it,
  When there is none to heal it,
  Nor numbed sense to steel it,
    Was never said in rhyme.

Happy is England! I could be content
    To see no other verdure than its own;
    To feel no other breezes than are blown
Through its tall woods with high romances blent:
Yet do I sometimes feel a languishment
    For skies Italian, and an inward groan
    To sit upon an Alp as on a throne,
And half forget what world or worldling meant.
Happy is England, sweet her artless daughters;
    Enough their simple loveliness for me,
        Enough their whitest arms in silence clinging:
    Yet do I often warmly burn to see
        Beauties of deeper glance, and hear their
            singing,
And float with them about the summer waters.

On First Looking into Chapman's Homer

Much have I travell'd in the realms of gold,
   And many goodly states and kingdoms seen;
   Round many western islands have I been
Which bards in fealty to Apollo hold.
Oft of one wide expanse had I been told
   That deep-brow'd Homer ruled as his demesne;
   Yet did I never breathe its pure serene
Till I heard Chapman speak out loud and bold:
Then felt I like some watcher of the skies
   When a new planet swims into his ken;
Or like stout Cortez when with eagle eyes
   He star'd at the Pacific – and all his men
Look'd at each other with a wild surmise –
   Silent, upon a peak in Darien.

On the Grasshopper and Cricket

The poetry of earth is never dead:
   When all the birds are faint with the hot sun,
   And hide in cooling trees, a voice will run
From hedge to hedge about the new-mown mead;
That is the Grasshopper's – he takes the lead
   In summer luxury, – he has never done
   With his delights; for when tired out with fun
He rests at ease beneath some pleasant weed.
The poetry of earth is ceasing never:
   On a lone winter evening, when the frost
     Has wrought a silence, from the stove there
     shrills
The Cricket's song, in warmth increasing ever,
   And seems to one in drowsiness half lost,
     The Grasshopper's among some grassy hills.

On the Sea

It keeps eternal whisperings around
  Desolate shores, and with its mighty swell
  Gluts twice ten thousand Caverns, till the spell
Of Hecate leaves them their old shadowy sound.
Often 'tis in such gentle temper found,
  That scarcely will the very smallest shell
  Be mov'd for days from where it sometime fell,
When last the winds of Heaven were unbound.
Oh ye! who have your eye-balls vex'd and tir'd,
  Feast them upon the wideness of the Sea;
    Oh ye! whose ears are dinn'd with uproar rude,
  Or fed too much with cloying melody –
    Sit ye near some old Cavern's Mouth and
      brood,
Until ye start, as if the sea-nymphs quir'd!

From ENDYMION: A Poetic Romance

Book 1

A thing of beauty is a joy for ever:
Its loveliness increases; it will never
Pass into nothingness; but still will keep
A bower quiet for us, and a sleep
Full of sweet dreams, and health, and quiet
    breathing.
Therefore, on every morrow, are we wreathing
A flowery band to bind us to the earth,
Spite of despondence, of the inhuman dearth
Of noble natures, of the gloomy days,
Of all the unhealthy and o'er-darkened ways
Made for our searching: yes, in spite of all,
Some shape of beauty moves away the pall
From our dark spirits. Such the sun, the moon,
Trees old, and young, sprouting a shady boon
For simple sheep; and such are daffodils
With the green world they live in; and clear rills
That for themselves a cooling covert make
'Gainst the hot season; the mid forest brake,
Rich with a sprinkling of fair musk-rose blooms:
And such too is the grandeur of the dooms
We have imagined for the mighty dead;
All lovely tales that we have heard or read:
An endless fountain of immortal drink,
Pouring unto us from the heaven's brink.

Nor do we merely feel these essences
For one short hour; no, even as the trees
That whisper round a temple become soon
Dear as the temple's self, so does the moon,
The passion poesy, glories infinite,
Haunt us till they become a cheering light
Unto our souls, and bound to us so fast,
That, whether there be shine, or gloom o'ercast,
They alway must be with us, or we die.

Therefore, 'tis with full happiness that I
Will trace the story of Endymion.
The very music of the name has gone
Into my being, and each pleasant scene
Is growing fresh before me as the green
Of our own vallies: so I will begin
Now while I cannot hear the city's din;
Now while the early budders are just new,
And run in mazes of the youngest hue
About old forests; while the willow trails
Its delicate amber; and the dairy pails
Bring home increase of milk. And, as the year
Grows lush in juicy stalks, I'll smoothly steer
My little boat, for many quiet hours,
With streams that deepen freshly into bowers.
Many and many a verse I hope to write,
Before the daisies, vermeil rimm'd and white,
Hide in deep herbage; and ere yet the bees
Hum about globes of clover and sweet peas,
I must be near the middle of my story.

O may no wintry season, bare and hoary,
See it half finish'd: but let Autumn bold,
With universal tinge of sober gold,
Be all about me when I make an end.
And now at once, adventuresome, I send
My herald thought into a wilderness:
There let its trumpet blow, and quickly dress
My uncertain path with green, that I may speed
Easily onward, thorough flowers and weed.

    Upon the sides of Latmos was outspread
A mighty forest; for the moist earth fed
So plenteously all weed-hidden roots
Into o'er-hanging boughs, and precious fruits.
And it had gloomy shades, sequestered deep,
Where no man went; and if from shepherd's keep
A lamb stray'd far a-down those inmost glens,
Never again saw he the happy pens
Whither his brethren, bleating with content,
Over the hills at every nightfall went.
Among the shepherds, 'twas believed ever,
That not one fleecy lamb which thus did sever
From the white flock, but pass'd unworried
By angry wolf, or pard with prying head,
Until it came to some unfooted plains
Where fed the herds of Pan; aye great his gains
Who thus one lamb did lose. Paths there were
    many,

Winding through palmy fern, and rushes fenny,
And ivy banks; all leading pleasantly
To a wide lawn, whence one could only see
Stems thronging all around between the swell
Of turf and slanting branches: who could tell
The freshness of the space of heaven above,
Edg'd round with dark tree tops? through which a
    dove
Would often beat its wings, and often too
A little cloud would move across the blue.

When I have fears that I may cease to be
   Before my pen has glean'd my teeming brain,
Before high-piled books, in charactery,
   Hold like rich garners the full ripen'd grain;
When I behold, upon the night's starr'd face,
   Huge cloudy symbols of a high romance,
And think that I may never live to trace
   Their shadows, with the magic hand of chance;
And when I feel, fair creature of an hour,
   That I shall never look upon thee more,
Never have relish in the faery power
   Of unreflecting love; – then on the shore
Of the wide world I stand alone, and think
Till love and fame to nothingness do sink.

From HYPERION:
A Fragment

Book 1

Deep in the shady sadness of a vale
Far sunken from the healthy breath of morn,
Far from the fiery noon, and eve's one star,
Sat gray-hair'd Saturn, quiet as a stone,
Still as the silence round about his lair;
Forest on forest hung about his head
Like cloud on cloud. No stir of air was there,
Not so much life as on a summer's day
Robs not one light seed from the feather'd grass,
But where the dead leaf fell, there did it rest.
A stream went voiceless by, still deadened more
By reason of his fallen divinity
Spreading a shade: the Naiad 'mid her reeds
Press'd her cold finger closer to her lips.

    Along the margin-sand large foot-marks went,
No further than to where his feet had stray'd,
And slept there since. Upon the sodden ground
His old right hand lay nerveless, listless, dead,
Unsceptred; and his realmless eyes were closed;
While his bow'd head seem'd list'ning to the
    Earth,
His ancient mother, for some comfort yet.

It seem'd no force could wake him from his
      place;
But there came one, who with a kindred hand
Touch'd his wide shoulders, after bending low
With reverence, though to one who knew it not.
She was a Goddess of the infant world;
By her in stature the tall Amazon
Had stood a pigmy's height: she would have ta'en
Achilles by the hair and bent his neck;
Or with a finger stay'd Ixion's wheel.
Her face was large as that of Memphian sphinx,
Pedestal'd haply in a palace court,
When sages look'd to Egypt for their lore.
But oh! how unlike marble was that face:

How beautiful, if sorrow had not made
Sorrow more beautiful than Beauty's self.
There was a listening fear in her regard,
As if calamity had but begun;
As if the vanward clouds of evil days
Had spent their malice, and the sullen rear
Was with its stored thunder labouring up.
One hand she press'd upon that aching spot
Where beats the human heart, as if just there,
Though an immortal, she felt cruel pain;
The other upon Saturn's bended neck
She laid, and to the level of his ear

Leaning with parted lips, some words she spake
In solemn tenour and deep organ tone;
Some mourning words, which in our feeble tongue
Would come in these like accents; O how frail
To that large utterance of the early Gods!
'Saturn, look up! – though wherefore, poor old
        King?
'I have no comfort for thee, no not one:
'I cannot say, "O wherefore sleepest thou?"
'For heaven is parted from thee, and the earth
'Knows thee not, thus afflicted, for a God;
'And ocean too, with all its solemn noise,
'Has from thy sceptre pass'd; and all the air
'Is emptied of thine hoary majesty.
'Thy thunder, conscious of the new command,
'Rumbles reluctant o'er our fallen house;
'And thy sharp lightning in unpractis'd hands
'Scorches and burns our once serene domain.
'O aching time! O moments big as years!
'All as ye pass swell out the monstrous truth,
'And press it so upon our weary griefs
'That unbelief has not a space to breathe.
'Saturn, sleep on: – O thoughtless, why did I
'Thus violate thy slumbrous solitude?
'Why should I ope thy melancholy eyes?
'Saturn, sleep on! while at thy feet I weep.'

As when, upon a tranced summer-night,
Those green-rob'd senators of mighty woods,
Tall oaks, branch-charmed by the earnest stars,
Dream, and so dream all night without a stir,
Save from one gradual solitary gust
Which comes upon the silence, and dies off,
As if the ebbing air had but one wave;
So came these words and went; the while in tears
She touch'd her fair large forehead to the ground,
Just where her falling hair might be outspread
A soft and silken mat for Saturn's feet.

Fancy

Ever let the fancy roam,
Pleasure never is at home;
At a touch sweet Pleasure melteth,
Like to bubbles when rain pelteth;
Then let winged Fancy wander
Through the thought still spread beyond her;
Open wide the mind's cage-door,
She'll dart forth, and cloudward soar,
O sweet Fancy! let her loose;
Summer's joys are spoilt by use,
And the enjoying of the Spring
Fades as does its blossoming;
Autumn's red-lipp'd fruitage too,
Blushing through the mist and dew,
Cloys with tasting: What do then?
Sit thee by the ingle, when
The sear faggot blazes bright,
Spirit of a winter's night;
When the soundless earth is muffled,
And the caked snow is shuffled
From the ploughboy's heavy shoon;
When the Night doth meet the Noon
In a dark conspiracy
To banish Even from her sky.
Sit thee there, and send abroad,
With a mind self-overaw'd,
Fancy, high-commission'd: – send her!

She has vassals to attend her:
She will bring, in spite of frost,
Beauties that the earth hath lost;
She will bring thee, all together,
All delights of summer weather;
All the buds and bells of May,
From dewy sward or thorny spray;
All the heaped Autumn's wealth,
With a still, mysterious stealth;
She will mix these pleasures up
Like three fit wines in a cup,
And thou shalt quaff it: – thou shalt hear
Distant harvest-carols clear;
Rustle of the reaped corn;
Sweet birds antheming the morn:
And, in the same moment – hark!
'Tis the early April lark,
Or the rooks, with busy caw,
Foraging for sticks and straw.
Thou shalt, at one glance, behold
The daisy and the marigold;
White-plum'd lillies, and the first
Hedge-grown primrose that hath burst;
Shaded hyacinth, alway
Sapphire queen of the mid-May;
And every leaf, and every flower
Pearled with the self-same shower.
Thou shalt see the field-mouse peep

Meagre from its celled sleep;
And the snake all winter-thin
Cast on sunny bank its skin;
Freckled nest-eggs thou shalt see
Hatching in the hawthorn-tree,
When the hen-bird's wing doth rest
Quiet on her mossy nest;
Then the hurry and alarm
When the bee-hive casts its swarm;
Acorns ripe down-pattering,
While the autumn breezes sing.

Oh, sweet Fancy! let her loose;
Every thing is spoilt by use:
Where's the cheek that doth not fade,
Too much gaz'd at? Where's the maid
Whose lip mature is ever new?
Where's the eye, however blue,
Doth not weary? Where's the face
One would meet in every place?
Where's the voice, however soft,
One would hear so very oft?
At a touch sweet Pleasure melteth
Like to bubbles when rain pelteth.
Let, then, winged Fancy find
Thee a mistress to thy mind:
Dulcet-eyed as Ceres' daughter,
Ere the God of Torment taught her

How to frown and how to chide;
With a waist and with a side
White as Hebe's, when her zone
Slipt its golden clasp, and down
Fell her kirtle to her feet,
While she held the goblet sweet,
And Jove grew languid. – Break the mesh
Of the Fancy's silken leash;
Quickly break her prison-string
And such joys as these she'll bring –
Let the winged Fancy roam,
Pleasure never is at home.

La Belle Dame sans Merci

I

O, what can ail thee, knight-at-arms,
    Alone and palely loitering?
The sedge has wither'd from the lake,
    And no birds sing.

II

O, what can ail thee, knight-at-arms,
    So haggard and so woe-begone?
The squirrel's granary is full,
    And the harvest's done.

III

I see a lilly on thy brow,
    With anguish moist and fever dew;
And on thy cheeks a fading rose
    Fast withereth too.

IV

I met a lady in the meads,
    Full beautiful – a faery's child,
Her hair was long, her foot was light,
    And her eyes were wild.

V

I made a garland for her head,
    And bracelets too, and fragrant zone;
She look'd at me as she did love,
    And made sweet moan.

VI

I set her on my pacing steed,
    And nothing else saw all day long;
For sidelong would she bend, and sing
    A faery's song.

VII

She found me roots of relish sweet,
    And honey wild, and manna dew,
And sure in language strange she said –
    'I love thee true'.

VIII

She took me to her elfin grot,
    And there she wept and sigh'd full sore,
And there I shut her wild wild eyes
    With kisses four.

IX

And there she lulled me asleep
    And there I dream'd – Ah! woe betide!
The latest dream I ever dream'd
    On the cold hill side.

X

I saw pale kings and princes too,
    Pale warriors, death-pale were they all;
They cried – 'La Belle Dame sans Merci
    Hath thee in thrall!'

XI

I saw their starved lips in the gloam,
    With horrid warning gaped wide,
And I awoke and found me here,
    On the cold hill's side

XII

And this is why I sojourn here
    Alone and palely loitering,
Though the sedge has wither'd from the lake,
    And no birds sing.

Ode to Psyche

O Goddess! hear these tuneless numbers, wrung
   By sweet enforcement and remembrance dear,
And pardon that thy secrets should be sung
   Even into thine own soft-conched ear:
Surely I dreamt to-day, or did I see
   The winged Psyche with awaken'd eyes?
I wander'd in a forest thoughtlessly,
   And, on the sudden, fainting with surprise,
Saw two fair creatures, couched side by side
   In deepest grass, beneath the whisp'ring roof
   Of leaves and trembled blossoms, where there
      ran
         A brooklet, scarce espied:

'Mid hush'd, cool-rooted flowers, fragrant-eyed,
   Blue, silver-white, and budded Tyrian,
They lay calm-breathing on the bedded grass;
   Their arms embraced, and their pinions too;
   Their lips touch'd not, but had not bade adieu,
As if disjoined by soft-handed slumber,
And ready still past kisses to outnumber
   At tender eye-dawn of aurorean love:
      The winged boy I knew;
   But who wast thou, O happy, happy dove?
      His Psyche true!

O latest born and loveliest vision far
    Of all Olympus' faded hierarchy!
Fairer than Phoebe's sapphire-region'd star,
    Or Vesper, amorous glow-worm of the sky;
Fairer than these, though temple thou hast none,
            Nor altar heap'd with flowers;
Nor virgin-choir to make delicious moan
            Upon the midnight hours;
No voice, no lute, no pipe, no incense sweet
    From chain-swung censer teeming;
No shrine, no grove, no oracle, no heat
    Of pale-mouth'd prophet dreaming.

O brightest! though too late for antique vows,
    Too, too late for the fond believing lyre,
When holy were the haunted forest boughs,
    Holy the air, the water, and the fire;
Yet even in these days so far retir'd
    From happy pieties, thy lucent fans,
    Fluttering among the faint Olympians,
I see, and sing, by my own eyes inspir'd.
So let me be thy choir, and make a moan
            Upon the midnight hours;
Thy voice, thy lute, thy pipe, thy incense sweet
    From swinged censer teeming;
Thy shrine, thy grove, thy oracle, thy heat
    Of pale-mouth'd prophet dreaming.

Yes, I will be thy priest, and build a fane
    In some untrodden region of my mind,
Where branched thoughts, new grown with
        pleasant pain,
    Instead of pines shall murmur in the wind:
Far, far around shall those dark-cluster'd trees
    Fledge the wild-ridged mountains steep by
        steep;
And there by zephyrs, streams, and birds, and
        bees,
    The moss-lain Dryads shall be lull'd to sleep;
And in the midst of this wide quietness
A rosy sanctuary will I dress
With the wreath'd trellis of a working brain,
    With buds, and bells, and stars without a name,
With all the gardener Fancy e'er could feign,
    Who breeding flowers, will never breed the
        same;
And there shall be for thee all soft delight
    That shadowy thought can win,
A bright torch, and a casement ope at night,
    To let the warm Love in!

Ode to a Nightingale

I

My heart aches, and a drowsy numbness pains
  My sense, as though of hemlock I had drunk,
Or emptied some dull opiate to the drains
  One minute past, and Lethe-wards had sunk:
'Tis not through envy of thy happy lot,
  But being too happy in thine happiness, –
    That thou, light-winged Dryad of the trees,
      In some melodious plot
  Of beechen green, and shadows numberless,
    Singest of summer in full-throated ease.

II

O, for a draught of vintage! that hath been
  Cool'd a long age in the deep-delved earth,
Tasting of Flora and the country green,
  Dance, and Provençal song, and sunburnt
      mirth!
O for a beaker full of the warm South,
  Full of the true, the blushful Hippocrene,
    With beaded bubbles winking at the brim,
      And purple-stained mouth;
  That I might drink, and leave the world
      unseen,
    And with thee fade away into the forest dim:

III

Fade far away, dissolve, and quite forget
    What thou among the leaves hast never known,
The weariness, the fever, and the fret
    Here, where men sit and hear each other groan;
Where palsy shakes a few, sad, last gray hairs,
    Where youth grows pale, and spectre-thin, and
        dies;
      Where but to think is to be full of sorrow
        And leaden-eyed despairs,
      Where Beauty cannot keep her lustrous eyes,
      Or new Love pine at them beyond
        to-morrow.

IV

Away! away! for I will fly to thee,
    Not charioted by Bacchus and his pards,
But on the viewless wings of Poesy,
    Though the dull brain perplexes and retards:
Already with thee! tender is the night,
    And haply the Queen-Moon is on her throne,
      Cluster'd around by all her starry Fays;
        But here there is no light,
Save what from heaven is with the breezes
      blown
      Through verdurous glooms and winding
        mossy ways.

V

I cannot see what flowers are at my feet,
  Nor what soft incense hangs upon the boughs,
But, in embalmed darkness, guess each sweet
  Wherewith the seasonable month endows
The grass, the thicket, and the fruit-tree wild;
  White hawthorn, and the pastoral eglantine;
    Fast fading violets cover'd up in leaves;
      And mid-May's eldest child,
The coming musk-rose, full of dewy wine,
    The murmurous haunt of flies on summer
      eves.

VI

Darkling I listen; and, for many a time
  I have been half in love with easeful Death,
Call'd him soft names in many a mused rhyme,
  To take into the air my quiet breath;
Now more than ever seems it rich to die,
  To cease upon the midnight with no pain,
    While though art pouring forth thy soul
      abroad
      In such an ecstasy!
  Still wouldst thou sing, and I have ears in
    vain –
    To thy high requiem become a sod.

VII

Thou wast not born for death, immortal Bird!
    No hungry generations tread thee down;
The voice I hear this passing night was heard
    In ancient days by emperor and clown:
Perhaps the self-same song that found a path
      Through the sad heart of Ruth, when, sick for
          home,
        She stood in tears amid the alien corn;
            The same that oft-times hath
      Charm'd magic casements, opening on the foam
      Of perilous seas, in faery lands forlorn.

VIII

Forlorn! the very word is like a bell
    To toll me back from thee to my sole self!
Adieu! the fancy cannot cheat so well
    As she is fam'd to do, deceiving elf.
Adieu! adieu! thy plaintive anthem fades
      Past the near meadows, over the still stream,
        Up the hill-side; and now 'tis buried deep
        In the next valley-glades:
    Was it a vision, or a waking dream?
      Fled is that music: – Do I wake or sleep?

Ode on a Grecian Urn

I

Thou still unravish'd bride of quietness,
   Thou foster-child of silence and slow time,
Sylvan historian, who canst thus express
   A flowery tale more sweetly than our rhyme:
What leaf-fring'd legend haunts about thy shape
   Of deities or mortals, or of both,
      In Tempe or the dales of Arcady?
   What men or gods are these? What maidens
      loth?
What mad pursuit? What struggle to escape?
     What pipes and timbrels? What wild ecstasy?

II

Heard melodies are sweet, but those unheard
   Are sweeter; therefore, ye soft pipes, play on;
Not to the sensual ear, but, more endear'd,
   Pipe to the spirit ditties of no tone:
Fair youth, beneath the trees, thou canst not
     leave
   Thy song, nor ever can those trees be bare;
     Bold Lover, never, never canst thou kiss,

Though winning near the goal – yet, do not
        grieve;
    She cannot fade, though thou hast not thy
        bliss,
        For ever wilt thou love, and she be fair!

III

Ah, happy, happy boughs! that cannot shed
    Your leaves, nor ever bid the Spring adieu;
And, happy melodist, unwearied,
    For ever piping songs for ever new;
More happy love! more happy, happy love!
    For ever warm and still to be enjoy'd,
        For ever panting, and for ever young;
All breathing human passion far above,
    That leaves a heart high-sorrowful and cloy'd,
        A burning forehead, and a parching tongue.

IV

Who are these coming to the sacrifice?
    To what green altar, O mysterious priest,
Lead'st thou that heifer lowing at the skies,
    And all her silken flanks with garlands drest?
What little town by river or sea shore,
    Or mountain-built with peaceful citadel,
        Is emptied of this folk, this pious morn?

And, little town, thy streets for evermore
    Will silent be; and not a soul to tell
        Why thou art desolate, can e'er return.

V

O Attic shape! Fair attitude! with brede
    Of marble men and maidens overwrought,
With forest branches and the trodden weed;
    Thou, silent form, dost tease us out of thought
As doth eternity: Cold Pastoral!
    When old age shall this generation waste,
        Thou shalt remain, in midst of other woe
Than ours, a friend to man, to whom thou say'st,
    'Beauty is truth, truth beauty,' – that is all
        Ye know on earth, and all ye need to know.

Bright star, would I were stedfast as thou art –
   Not in lone splendour hung aloft the night
And watching, with eternal lids apart,
   Like nature's patient, sleepless Eremite,
The moving waters at their priestlike task
   Of pure ablution round earth's human shores,
Or grazing on the new soft-fallen mask
   Of snow upon the mountains and the moors –
No – yet still stedfast, still unchangeable,
   Pillow'd upon my fair love's ripening breast,
To feel for ever its soft fall and swell,
   Awake for ever in a sweet unrest,
Still, still to hear her tender-taken breath,
And so live ever – or else swoon to death.

Ode on Melancholy

I

No, no, go not to Lethe, neither twist
 Wolf's-bane, tight-rooted, for its poisonous
  wine;
Nor suffer thy pale forehead to be kiss'd
 By nightshade, ruby grape of Proserpine;
Make not your rosary of yew-berries,
 Nor let the beetle, nor the death-moth be
  Your mournful Psyche, nor the downy owl
A partner in your sorrow's mysteries;
 For shade to shade will come too drowsily,
  And drown the wakeful anguish of the soul.

II

But when the melancholy fit shall fall
 Sudden from heaven like a weeping cloud,
That fosters the droop-headed flowers all,
 And hides the green hill in an April shroud;
Then glut thy sorrow on a morning rose,
 Or on the rainbow of the salt sand-wave,
  Or on the wealth of globed peonies;
Or if thy mistress some rich anger shows,
 Emprison her soft hand, and let her rave,
  And feed deep, deep upon her peerless eyes.

III

She dwells with Beauty – Beauty that must die;
    And Joy, whose hand is ever at his lips
Bidding adieu; and aching Pleasure nigh,
    Turning to Poison while the bee-mouth sips:
Ay, in the very temple of delight
    Veil'd Melancholy has her sovran shrine,
      Though seen of none save him whose
        strenuous tongue
    Can burst Joy's grape against his palate fine;
His soul shall taste the sadness of her might,
      And be among her cloudy trophies hung.

To Autumn

I

Season of mists and mellow fruitfulness,
   Close bosom-friend of the maturing sun;
Conspiring with him how to load and bless
   With fruit the vines that round the thatch-eves
      run;
To bend with apples the moss'd cottage-trees,
   And fill all fruit with ripeness to the core;
     To swell the gourd, and plump the hazel
      shells
   With a sweet kernel; to set budding more,
And still more, later flowers for the bees,
Until they think warm days will never cease,
     For Summer has o'er-brimm'd their clammy
      cells.

II

Who hath not seen thee oft amid thy store?
   Sometimes whoever seeks abroad may find
Thee sitting careless on a granary floor,
   Thy hair soft-lifted by the winnowing wind;
Or on a half-reap'd furrow sound asleep,

Drows'd with the fume of poppies, while thy
     hook
     Spares the next swath and all its twined
          flowers:
And sometimes like a gleaner thou dost keep
     Steady thy laden head across a brook;
     Or by a cyder-press, with patient look,
          Thou watchest the last oozings hours by
          hours.

III

Where are the songs of Spring? Ay, where are
     they?
     Think not of them, thou hast thy music too, –
While barred clouds bloom the soft-dying day,
     And touch the stubble-plains with rosy hue;
Then in a wailful choir the small gnats mourn
     Among the river sallows, borne aloft
          Or sinking as the light wind lives or dies;
And full-grown lambs loud bleat from hilly bourn;
     Hedge-crickets sing; and now the treble soft
     The red-breast whistles from a garden-croft;
          And gathering swallows twitter in the skies.

This living hand, now warm and capable
Of earnest grasping, would, if it were cold
And in the icy silence of the tomb,
So haunt thy days and chill thy dreaming nights
That thou wouldst wish thine own heart dry of
      blood
So in my veins red life might stream again,
And thou be conscience-calm'd – see here it is –
I hold it towards you.

NOTES ON THE PICTURES

p. 6   *John Keats* by Joseph Severn (1793–1879). National Portrait Gallery, London.

p. 15   *The Vale of Dedham* by John Constable (1776–1837). National Gallery of Scotland, Edinburgh.

p. 19   *Farewell to the Black Sea* by Ivan K. Aivazovsky (1817–1900). Photo: Fine Art Photographic Library, London.

p. 23   *Diana and Endymion* by Hugh Douglas Hamilton (1739–1808). Christie's, London. Photo: Bridgeman Art Library, London.

p. 27   *The Colossus* by Francisco Goya (1746–1828). Bibliothèque Nationale, Paris.

p. 34   *Clouds* by John Constable (1776–1837). Reproduced by courtesy of the Board of Trustees of the Victoria and Albert Museum, London.

p. 39   *La Belle Dame sans Merci* by Sir Frank Dicksee (1853–1928). City of Bristol Museum and Art Gallery.

p. 43   *Psyche Receiving her First Kiss from the God Love* by François Pascal Simon Gerard (1770–1837). Louvre, Paris.

p. 47   *Bacchus and Ariadne* by Vecelli Titian (1477/89–1575). National Gallery, London.

p. 51   *Amphore Apulienne* from *Histoire de La Céramique Grecque* by Olivier Rayet and Maxime Collignon, Paris, 1888.

p. 55   *The Rainbow* by George Frederick Watts (1817–1904). Fine Art Society, London.

p. 58   *Still Life of Melons, Grapes and Peaches on a Ledge* by Jakob Bogdany (1660–1724). Johnny Van Haeften Gallery, London. Photo: Bridgeman Art Library, London.

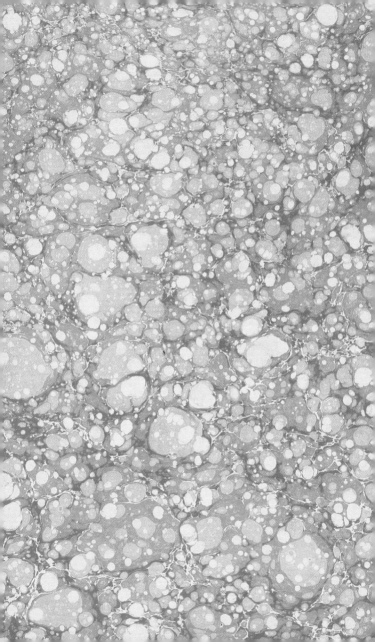